Truly Foul & Cheesy™
Space
Facts
& Jokes

Published in Great Britain in MMXIX by
Book House, an imprint of
The Salariya Book Company Ltd
25 Marlborough Place, Brighton BN1 1UB
www.salariya.com

ISBN: 978-1-912537-37-2

1 3 5 7 9 8 6 4 2

A CIP catalogue record for this book is available
from the British Library.

Printed and bound in China.
Printed on paper from sustainable sources.

Author:
John Townsend worked as a
secondary school teacher before
becoming a full-time writer.
He specialises in illuminating and
humorous information books for
all ages.

Artist:
David Antram studied at
Eastbourne College of Art and then
worked in advertising for 15 years
before becoming a full-time artist.
He has illustrated many children's
non-fiction books.

Truly Foul & Cheesy™ Space Facts & Jokes

This Truly Foul & Cheesy book belongs to:

....

Written by
John Townsend

Illustrated by
David Antram

BOOK HOUSE
a SALARIYA imprint

Introduction

Warning – reading this book might not make you **LOL** (laugh out loud), but it could make you **GOL** (groan out loud), feel sick out loud or **SEL** (scream even louder). If you are reading this in a library by a **SILENCE** sign… get ready to be thrown out!

Disclaimer: The author really hasn't made anything up in this book (apart from some daft limericks and jokes).

He checked out the foul facts as best he could and even double-checked the fouler bits to make sure – so please don't get too upset if you find out something different from a passing astronaut or a cosmonaut (Russian). If you come face to face with a taikonaut (Chinese space traveller) or a spationaut (European), you're probably lost anyway. If you come face to face with a juggernaut, step out the way fast!

If I had my way, I'd RATiFY the lot!

Official

warning

This book is a cosmic mix of wow information that's out of this world – far beyond planet Earth. With a few gross and toe-curling facts thrown in, it will hurtle you through space, with a real risk of making you grossed-out now and again. That's normal. Most astronauts get space sick – mainly from zero gravity, rather than from cheesy jokes of zero quality. So, hold on to your back ear (as you head to the final front-ear) and get ready for blast-off… as you boldly go into the foul and cheesy beyond. You have been warned…

Space travel limerick

If you go on a superpowered flight
In a rocket that's faster than light,
Be sure your pyjamas
Are ready for dramas...
Like returning the previous night.

Riddles

First up – time to get 6 cheesy riddles out of the way...

Q: Why does a Moon rock taste better than an Earth rock?
A: It's a little meteor.

Q: How many aerospace engineers does it take to set off your bonfire night party?
A: None, you don't have to be a rocket scientist to light a firework.

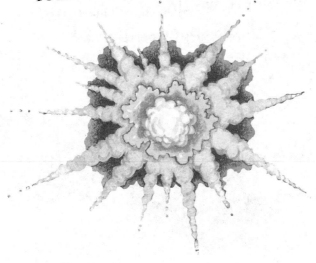

Q: How do you get a baby astronaut to sleep?
A: You rocket.

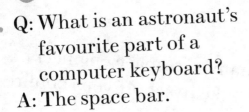

Q: What is an astronaut's
favourite part of a
computer keyboard?
A: The space bar.

Q: Where would an astronaut
park his space ship?
A: A parking meteor!

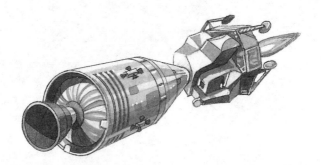

Q: How does one astronaut on the
Moon tell another astronaut that
he is sorry?
A: He Apollo-gises.

In Case you'd forgotten...

Everything on Earth – including us – is held down by the force of gravity. Without gravity, we would all float off into space. Isaac Newton (1643-1727) discovered all about gravity (and bruises) when an apple fell on his head and got him thinking.

Rockets need huge amounts of fuel for the energy to overcome Earth's gravity. Only when they reach a speed of over 27,358 kilometres per hour (17,000 miles per hour) are rockets fast enough to enter orbit.

Most rockets are made up of two or three stages. When a stage has used up its fuel, it is ejected to get rid of the dead weight. It then falls back (usually into the ocean and far from populated areas) or burns up in the atmosphere. Scientists have even been studying the use of powerful magnets to send a spacecraft into orbit. Maybe 'electromagnetic propulsion' will power rockets in the future.

A quick history of rockets

to get us off the ground

Rockets have been around a long time. They were invented in China, more than 800 years ago, as simple tubes packed with gunpowder and attached to a guide stick – similar to the fireworks we use today.

These would make whizzo weapons.

In 1232, the Chinese used these 'fire arrows' to defeat the invading Mongol army.

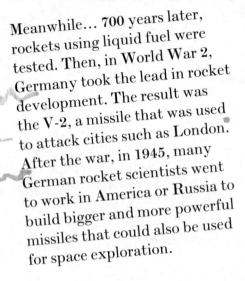

Meanwhile… 700 years later, rockets using liquid fuel were tested. Then, in World War 2, Germany took the lead in rocket development. The result was the V-2, a missile that was used to attack cities such as London. After the war, in 1945, many German rocket scientists went to work in America or Russia to build bigger and more powerful missiles that could also be used for space exploration.

Sputnik 1, the world's first satellite, was about the size of a beach ball and took about 98 minutes to orbit the Earth. It was launched by a Russian rocket in 1957. Within 10 years, the United States was close to building a craft that could carry three men to the Moon.

Light the blue touch paper and stand clear

For centuries people dreamed of travelling up through the clouds to other worlds. In the last century, as rocket science developed, it became possible to fire machines higher and higher. In the late 1950s, the 'space race' really took off – as Russia and the USA competed to get the first manned space flight off the ground.

But did they know it had already been done? At least, according to an old Chinese story, someone had already been blasted into the clouds. In the 16th century, a Chinese official named Wan-Hu apparently made a rocket-powered flying chair. After all, the Chinese had been making gunpowder for centuries, and using firework rockets. Wan-Hu's chair was attached to two wooden posts, with large kites fixed above and forty-seven fire-arrow rockets underneath.

Wan-Hu sat in the chair and gave the command to light the rockets. Forty-seven assistants, each with a fire-torch, stepped forward and lit the rockets. In a flash and a roar, the chair disappeared in a cloud of smoke. When the smoke cleared, Wan-Hu and his flying chair were gone. No one knows what happened to Wan-Hu, but maybe he's still up there somewhere! (Not so much Wan-Hu as Wan-Where?)

Yikes - I forgot to fit brakes!

Cue for a limerick:

As Wan-Hu sat strapped in his chair
And the gunpowder started to flare,
He shrugged, 'This appliance
Is not rocket science.'
In a flash he was no longer there!
(Disappeared, it seemed, into thin air.)

Big discovery

Galileo Galilei (1564–1642) was an Italian scientist who opened the eyes of the world to how our solar system works. That was vital information when it came to planning future space missions. Using his own invented telescope, Galileo looked far into space and was the first to see Jupiter's moons and the craters on our Moon. But he also realised how the Earth and other planets moved around the Sun and not the other way around, as used to be thought. In fact, the Catholic church was so cross with Galileo for teaching that we (Earth) weren't at the centre of the universe, that he was arrested and forbidden to teach, write or leave his house. No friends could come for sleep-overs, either.

Of course, he was right all along and 350 years later, the Pope said sorry and gave Galileo a pardon. Someone should have said sorry about his finger, too. When he died, someone cut off Galileo's finger to put on display at a museum in Florence, Italy. Maybe it should be sticking up to the sky with the label: 'Galileo Galilei had a good point.'

First into space

In the early days of real rocket science, no one knew what the effects of weightlessness would be on humans. So, animals were used to test the safety of launching a living creature into space and bringing it back unharmed. Sadly, things didn't always go well.

Tissues at the ready

In 1957, just one month after all the excitement of Sputnik 1's success, Russia (then known as the Soviet Union) launched Sputnik 2 with the first living passenger, a stray dog called Laika. What people weren't told at the time (look away now if you're a dog lover as it gets nasty) was that poor Laika overheated and died five hours into the space flight.

Many animals have continued to head for the stars. In 1960 Russia launched Sputnik 5, which carried the dogs Belka and Strelka, along with a rabbit, 40 mice, 2 rats and 15 flasks of fruit flies and plants. It was the first spacecraft to carry animals into orbit and return them alive.

I never want to be a rat-stronaut. It's not so much a space race as a rat race.

Astronauts have studied all kinds
of animals in space. Did you know
all of these have been launched?
Monkeys, cats, dogs, wasps,
beetles, tortoises, flies, worms, fish,
spiders, rabbits, bees, ants, frogs,
mice, crickets, rats, newts, snails,
urchins, moths, shrimps, jellyfish,
guinea pigs, butterflies, scorpions
and cockroaches. Luckily, they
didn't all go up at once – and many
returned to Earth alive and well.

Animal stars of the stars

Ham, a chimpanzee, trained to perform tasks during spaceflight in 1961. He learned to pull levers to receive banana pellets and avoid electric shocks (a useful trick!). He successfully became the first animal to 'interact' with a space vessel rather than just ride in it. Maybe he was trying to say 'Get me out of here!'

In 1963, French scientists launched the first cat into space. Felix was successfully retrieved after a parachute descent. He was CATegorical he didn't want to go back!

In 1966 two Russian dogs, Veterok and Ugolyok, were launched into space and orbited Earth for a record-breaking 22 days. Humans did not beat their record until 1974.

Foul fact

(if you don't like creepy crawlies floating around your face)

The European Space Agency in 2007 launched into space a cockroach, which became the first creature to give birth somewhere other than on Earth. Another 33 cockroaches were found inside the sealed container when the spacecraft returned to Earth.

Six firsts:

1 The first space traveller was Soviet cosmonaut Yuri Gagarin (1934–1968), who orbited the Earth in 1961, aboard Vostok 1. He died in a training crash 7 years later.

2 Later in 1961, Alan Shepard became the first U.S. astronaut to travel into space when he was launched aboard Freedom 7 and flew at 187 kilometres (116 miles) above the Earth.

3 Apollo 14 astronaut Alan Shepard was the first person to play golf on the Moon. It's estimated that the ball travelled for over 1.6 kilometres (over a mile), unofficially setting the record for the longest drive in history.

In 1963, Russian cosmonaut Valentina Tereshkova became the first woman in space when she flew aboard Vostok 6.

 In 1983, Sally Ride became the first U.S. astronaut to fly in space, aboard Space Shuttle Challenger.

 In 1995 Norman Thagard became the first U.S. astronaut to become a cosmonaut too, when he flew onboard the Soyuz spacecraft for Russia's Mir-18 mission.

Silly riddle time

Q: What do you call a baby cosmonaut?
A: Yuri Googoogagarin.

Q: How do astronauts organise
a space mission?
A: They planet.

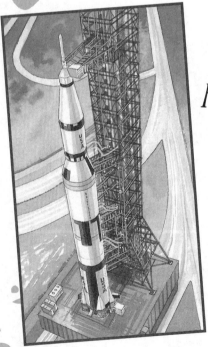

Q: What time do
astronauts eat?
A: At launch time.

Q: What is a black hole?
A: What an astronaut gets in a black sock.

Q: What's E.T. short for?
A: Because he's only got little legs (Extra Terrestrial = beyond Earth).

For the record

Well over 550 people have flown in space so far – many of them taking several trips.

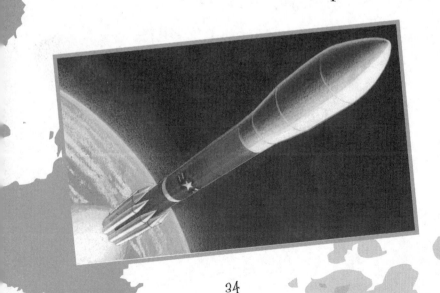

In 1994–1995 Valeri Polyakov spent nearly 438 days in space – that's over 1 year and 2 months without a plate of chips.

So far 12 people have walked on the Moon. Who will dare to be the 13th?!

Risky rockets

Before you consider becoming the next person to walk on the Moon, you might need to consider the risks. Space travel has a history of danger.

So far there have been 18 astronaut and cosmonaut deaths during spaceflights. Other astronauts have died while training for space missions, such as the Apollo 1 launch pad fire which killed an entire crew of three in 1967.

Two of the worst **NASA** disasters (and most expensive) entered the record books. (NASA = USA's National Aeronautics and Space Administration)

1986 Challenger Explosion

The American shuttle orbiter Challenger broke up 73 seconds after lift-off, bringing a devastating end to the spacecraft's 10th mission. The disaster claimed the lives of all seven astronauts aboard. A faulty seal leaked gas, which ignited and caused a massive explosion. The whole event was seen by millions on live TV around the world. The cost of replacing the Space Shuttle was $2 billion. The cost of the investigation and replacement of lost equipment cost $450 million from 1986–1987 ($1 billion in today's dollars).

2003 Space Shuttle Columbia

When re-entering the Earth's atmosphere over Texas, the space shuttle Columbia suddenly broke apart, killing all seven crew members on board. The disaster was caused when the shuttle launched the month before. A piece of foam insulation had broken away and damaged the shuttle's wing. Finding out exactly what went wrong cost $300 million but the final cost of the accident came to a staggering $13 billion.

How to become an astronaut

So now you know some of the risks, would you fancy travelling into space? If you'd like to apply to be an astronaut, you'll need to know a few more facts. Brace yourself...

First up...

Astronauts need to train for 2 years straight after being selected for a programme.

To become an astronaut with NASA, you need to become a U.S. citizen.

NASA selects candidates to become astronauts every 2 years.

Tough
Competition

In 2017, more than 18,000 people applied to join NASA's astronaut class. Very few were selected! It was the same in the early days. One NASA astronaut waited 19 years to fly in space. Don Lind was selected in 1966, but was chosen for cancelled missions or as a reserve crew member, so he never got off the ground. He said, 'I was backing up two of the most depressingly healthy people you can imagine.' Lind finally flew on the space shuttle in 1985.

Did you know?

NASA has strict requirements for being an astronaut. You must be in top physical shape (that means having a very scary medical), as well as have a 'technical brain' to take on difficult jobs in a spacecraft or on a space station far from home. You need a degree in engineering, biological science, physical science, computer science or mathematics, followed by three years of professional experience (or 1,000 hours of pilot-in-command experience in jet aircraft). You'll also need to demonstrate your skills at scuba diving, wilderness experience, leadership expertise and the ability to read and speak Russian.
Still interested? Try this...

Foul alert

Astronaut recruits get training in a specially
fitted aircraft that uses a flight method
called parabolic flight. That basically
throws you around and creates a weightless
environment for 20-25 second intervals. The
exercise puts strain on the body, making one
out of every three astronauts sick – earning the
nickname 'the vomit comet'.

What will happen if you survive the Vomit Comet?

Firstly, new astronauts might travel up to the International Space Station (ISS), about 322 kilometres (200 miles) above the Earth. You'd get to glimpse home several times a day as the ISS is travelling at around 28,164 kilometres per hour (17,500 miles per hour) and orbits the Earth every 90 minutes.

Five fast facts on the ISS:

 On average, the ISS sees 16 sunrises and sunsets per 24 hours.

 The ISS provides more living room than an average six-bedroom house.

3 The Olympic torch has even made its way to the Space Station and went outside into space on a spacewalk.

4 Inside the ISS, there are two bathrooms, a gym and a 360-degree-view bay window.

5 The ISS can be seen from Earth with the naked eye and is the largest artificial satellite that has ever orbited our planet.

What next?

The International Space Station (15 countries are involved in its operations) was originally due to last until 2024, but it could be extended until 2028 or longer. But if you'd still like to be a space-traveller after then, NASA has future projects in the pipeline (or on the launchpad). It is testing its Orion spacecraft, which is expected to make an un-crewed flight past the Moon in 2019. Orion is planned to carry humans to deep-space destinations in the 2020s and beyond. Trips to Mars are on the cards in the 2030s – so book your place soon!

Or book an 'out of this world' wedding!

Can you believe it?

In 2003, Yuri Malenchenko (from Ukraine) married his fiancée Ekaterina Dmitriev (U.S.) over 322 kilometres (200 miles) up in space. Their marriage was performed over a video conference link between the bride in Houston, Texas and the groom who was commanding the Expedition 7 mission in the International Space Station. All in a day's work!

Cue for a joke:

Did you hear about the two astronauts who got married on a radio satellite dish in space? It wasn't much of a ceremony (not much atmosphere), but with such a strong signal from Earth, the reception was brilliant! They even took a beehive, so they could have a real honeymoon.

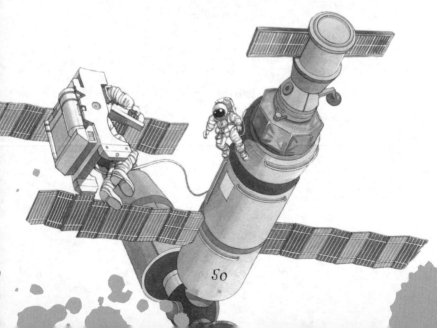

Joking astronauts

NASA astronaut Owen Garriott played a joke on controllers down on the ground by playing a recording of his wife whilst on Skylab. There were no women on board the space station and he fooled everyone into thinking there was a stowaway on board.

Apollo 12 commander Pete Conrad's first word when setting foot on the Moon was 'Whoopee!' so he could win a $500 bet with an Italian journalist that NASA didn't script what astronauts could say.

Joking

Cosmonaut

An astronaut and a cosmonaut are sitting together in the International Space Station.

Cosmonaut: You know, comrade, we Russians were the first to go to space.

Astronaut: Well, that may be true, buddy, but we Americans were the first to land on the Moon.

Cosmonaut: Then I bet we will be the first to land on the Sun

Astronaut: Gee – however you gonna do that without burning to a frazzle?

Cosmonaut: Simple – we will go at night (winks).

Astronaut: Doh!

Why don't astronauts or cosmonauts keep their jobs very long?
Because as soon as they start they get fired.

A Russian cosmonaut crash landed in the Great Red Desert of Australia and woke up in a daze inside a white room. As his eyes opened, he looked up at the ceiling, trying to figure out where on Earth he was. After a few moments, the face of a doctor appeared above him. She smiled warmly as, still stunned, he managed to croak in his best English (the international language), 'Did you bring me here to die?'

The doctor looked down into his pleading eyes and touched his cold hand.

'No, mate, we brought you here yes-te-die.'

Did you know that **NASA** is giving a lecture on time travel? It will be held last Tuesday.

Life in space

Warning – things are about to get FOUL (and sometimes fouler)

Many people dream of being able to travel and live in space. The excitement, adventure and wonder of manned space travel have kept astronauts the subject of great interest for sixty years. But it's not all glamour up there with the stars. Now it's time to talk about the yuckier bits…

Something you should know to begin with...

1 In space, low gravity makes it difficult to tell if your bladder is full. The bladder's stretch receptor nerves don't feel the weight of the liquid, so you don't get the signal that you need to pee. Astronauts are trained to empty their bladders every two hours, otherwise... no doubt you can imagine.

Astronauts must have good airflow around them when they sleep, otherwise they could wake up oxygen-deprived and gasping for air because a bubble of their own exhaled carbon dioxide has formed around their heads. Modern space craft are well-equipped for good ventilation and air supply.

Sneezing in a space suit is a dodgy business. Astronauts must lean their heads forward and sneeze into their chests to prevent gooey mucus from splattering all over their visor. When a person coughs or sneezes on Earth, the particles blast 1–2 metres away before gravity knocks them out of the air. In space, the snotty cloud will disperse all around, so germs could spread quickly.

But what if you suffer from hay fever? Believe it or not, the second American in space had hay fever and was about to be disqualified from astronaut training until NASA realised you can't get hay fever in space as there's no pollen to trigger it.

Foul limerick time

An astronaut at the space station
Made a somewhat profound
observation:
If you sneeze without gravity,
Your complete nasal cavity
Clogs up – before regurgitation!

Eating

In the early days of space travel, astronauts had to make do with dull food in dried cubes or squeezing goo from containers like toothpaste tubes. The lack of room for storage and the risk of spilling fluids or crumbs meant meals were limited. This has now changed in the space station, where there is plenty of room to prepare more interesting meals.

Most space dinners today involve adding water to such delights as macaroni or spaghetti – and now an oven in the space station can cook a lot of the dishes just like at home. Even so, there are no big refrigerators in space, so fresh food has limited storage. And the problem is, you can't call for a take-away in space. Not many pizza delivery companies have their own rockets. One thing you never hear an astronaut say: 'Shall we eat out tonight?'

Salt and pepper are carried in spacecraft, but only in a liquid form. If astronauts sprinkled salt and pepper on their food in space, it would simply float away and maybe clog the air vents. Pepper flying around could get in an astronaut's eyes or fly up everyone's noses. That could start a lot of messy sneezing – with truly disgusting results.

Space trash

As space food comes in disposable packages, astronauts must throw their plastic packaging away when they finish eating. The proper disposal of rubbish and plastic has become a problem. Just throwing waste out of spaceships has made a lot of space junk, which can be a danger to spacecraft and orbiting satellites. There's now a lot of mess floating around in space, probably including half-eaten pizzas, apple cores and leftover spaghetti.

Lunar Picnic

Neil Armstrong and Buzz Aldrin, the first astronauts to land on the Moon in 1969, had bacon cubes as part of their first meal on the Moon. The full meal included four bacon cubes, three sugar cookies, peaches, pineapple-grapefruit drink and coffee.

Did you know?

The Moon is littered with rubbish from when Apollo astronauts walked across its surface. Everything from dirty pants, food waste, old equipment, probes, flags and footprints were left behind – almost 200 tons of rubbish. If you ever decide to go to the Moon, be careful where you tread. Astronauts left plenty of other waste from emptied toilets, too. It will never rot away on the Moon where there are no bacteria to clear it up. As far as we know, there are no 'lunar garbage collectors' – yet.

Drinking

Slurping liquids in microgravity can be tricky – usually involving sucking from a squelchy bag through a straw. The International Space Station has tested special cups that allow astronauts to drink more normally. The splash-free Space Cups use surface tension and a clever design to stop liquid escaping and floating off to cause havoc with the electrics.

Sleeping

How can you sleep without gravity to keep you on the bed? Astronauts have to strap themselves to a bunk or use a sleeping bag that is fastened to a wall, so they don't float around and bump into things while they're asleep. 'Drifting off to sleep' is literally true if you're not tied down!

Washing

As water needs gravity to flow, showers in space are different from home. Astronauts must shower in an enclosed cylinder to keep water from floating away. They wash their hair with no-rinse shampoo, spray themselves with a nozzle to rinse off and use a vacuum hose attachment to suck up all the water from their skin. A good soak in a bathtub is out of the question.

Smelly space

According to astronaut Scott Kelly, the space station smells like jail – a mix of 'antiseptic, garbage and body odour'. While touring a jail in Texas, Kelly said he got a whiff in one room that reminded him of his days on the ISS. Although astronauts use deodorant and they shower on board, the smell of body odour can still linger in spacecraft. Residents of the ISS only change their socks and underwear every other day, and shirts every 10 days. That might seem gross but clothes don't get as dirty in space as they do on Earth.

3...2...1... we have pants off!

Russian scientists have thought a lot about the problem of dirty underwear in space. That's because smelly pants have to sit on the Space Station for months at a time. Scientists have come up with a system to use bacteria for digesting the astronauts' used cotton and paper underwear. Apart from making unwanted pants biodegrade (that's polite for 'rot away'), they think the gas that bacteria make could be used to help fuel the spacecraft. It seems research looking into undies is still in progress – that really is a job that must be **PANTS.**

Foul pants and cheesy socks

Another fact about pants in space might surprise you. Dirty underwear and toilet paper have helped to grow plants on the International Space Station. American astronaut Don Pettit discovered that by folding a pair of underpants into a sphere shape and stitching in some Russian toilet paper (which is thick wool-like gauze), this created a warmer environment for tomato and basil seeds to sprout. Astronauts' dirty socks can also provide extra nutrients for tomato seeds to sprout in and grow. Maybe the final fruit is cheese and tomato flavoured.

Toilets

The big question: how do you go to the toilet in space? Engineers have designed various toilets with tubes, funnels and vacuum pumps, but with the purpose of recycling urine so it can be drunk again and again.

Having enough fresh water can be a big problem in space. Astronauts at the International Space Station get most of their water by recycling and recovering it using the Water Recovery System, which NASA introduced in 2009. This allows astronauts to recover most of the water they lose through sweat and urine. American astronauts don't just recycle their own urine. They're also recycling the urine of Russian cosmonauts, who refuse to recycle their own pee. According to NASA's water manager for the ISS, the recycled water tastes just like bottled water. Fancy a wee drop?

Poo-ston, we have a problem...

In 1981, astronauts John Young and Robert Crippen piloted the Space Shuttle Columbia on its maiden mission, but something foul bubbled up. The toilet clogged, forcing the two men to use special tube-shaped bags sealed to their bottoms for holding poo. Yes, a kind of space nappy! If you prefer the technical term, these were 'faecal containment systems'. Look out – it gets worse... During re-entry, vacuum-dried poo from the broken toilet got sucked into the ventilation system and entered the main cabin. Young and Crippen had to dodge the poop particles and smile sweetly for the cameras as they stepped from the craft. Normally, space toilets work well, but instead of flushing with water, they use air to blow away waste into a storage tank. This gets emptied into space at regular intervals. Look out for UFOs... Unidentified Foul Objects.

Loo-pee limerick

If you ever go up into space,
Take a lavatory brush, just in case
The loo in the rocket
Needs your skill to unblock it
Before it erupts in your face.

Itchy scratchy

A problem when wearing a spacesuit is trying to scratch an itch. According to one astronaut, it can take a lot of wriggling with plenty of 'shake, rattle and roll' to reach an itch. But what if the itch is on your face inside the space helmet? The answer is to rub your itchy face against a piece of Velcro stuck on the inside.

Yikes - in a RASH moment I cut my fingernails.

The problem with scratching is that tiny skin cells flake off. On Earth gravity makes these fall to the ground as dust. In space there's no gravity to pull the dead cells away so they float all over the spacecraft. With many astronauts living together on a space station at the same time, they must cope with floating clouds of dead skin wafting all over the place. Gross.

A Dalek burst into the space station blaring 'EXFOLIATE'.

Foul alert:

Calluses are areas of hard, thickened skin that develop from pressure on the body or the rubbing of clothes. Astronaut Scott Kelly said, 'The calluses on your feet in space will eventually fall off, so the bottoms of your feet become very soft, like a baby's feet. But the top of my feet developed rough alligator skin because I used the top of my feet to get around the space station when using foot rails.' Floating calluses in a spaceship could easily clog up equipment or (brace yourself) drift into the open mouth of anyone aboard. Extra gross!

Gas and worse

Believe it or not, 'bottom gas' was a major safety concern early in the space programme. Scientists were afraid that flammable methane gas in farts could be explosive. NASA spent a lot of time and money on studies to find a way to prevent this from happening. Today the ISS and spacesuits are fitted with filters that remove these gases whenever an astronaut breaks wind. Baked beans aren't advised on a space trip.

More
space wind

Everyone burps from time to time – even
astronauts… although they must try not to.
Burping in space can turn nasty as there is no
gravity to separate liquid from gas inside stomachs.
As the stomach breaks down food, it produces
gas, which normally rises up through the mouth.
In space, gases stay trapped in the stomach. Any
attempt to burp can result in vomiting. Vomit-
proof belches take a lot of practice to get right.
You can imagine how nasty floating vomit must be
in a spacecraft. If an astronaut feels sick, it's time to
reach for a barf bag. These containers have zip locks
which prevent the waste from floating around the
$100 billion orbiting laboratory and splattering it.

Extra foul alert

The Apollo 8 mission prepared the way of the eventual Moon landing of Apollo 11. It was commanded by Frank Borman who felt rather unwell mid-flight. Houston, he had a problem. He woke from a nap with an upset stomach. He vomited and had diarrhoea, the globules of which floated all over the inside of the space craft in zero gravity. It took so much cleaning, he was completely spaced out – groan.

Feeling ill

Nearly every astronaut has suffered from space sickness. The symptoms are headaches, nausea and vomiting into the barf bag. However much they train for the rigours of space travel, 80% of astronauts experience SAS (space adaptation syndrome) when they come back to Earth. Their brains are confused by the change of atmosphere and adjusting to gravity once more. That can mean feeling unwell, dizzy and clumsy, including dropping objects because things are now so heavy after being light and 'floaty' in space. Yes, it's back to Earth with a bump – or several.

Sweating

We all sweat and astronauts in space are no different – except they *are* slightly different. That's because their sweat actually sticks to their bodies, instead of evaporating. The sweaty blobs can gather in pools over the skin and can easily run into the eyes. When astronauts do their exercises on the ISS, the sweat often flings off their bodies and sticks to the walls of the station. If they find that upsetting, it's best not to cry. The tears do not fall, they just stay on the astronaut's face and form a blob around the eyes. It's no use crying about it – it will just get worse!

Bleeding

Accidents are bound to happen in space but how does the body react to a cut? During spaceflight, thanks to surface tension, the blood that seeps from a cut pools and forms a dome over the wound. This dome will stay on an astronaut's body until a force acts on it to push it away. Then it could float all over the place and join all that sweat sticking to the walls. Do you still want to be an astronaut?

Silly story
(fake news)

Scientists at **NASA** have developed a special kind of cannon that fires dead chickens at the windshields of the space shuttle and other spacecraft flying at full speed. The aim is to study the effects of collisions with airborne fowl and to test the strength of the windshields. The problem of aircraft flying into flocks of birds has also been a concern of British engineers. They heard about **NASA**'s cannon and were eager to test it on the windscreens of jet aircraft.

When **NASA** loaned their cannon, the British engineers were shocked when the first chicken fired from the barrel and crashed into the shatterproof shield. It smashed it to smithereens, crashed through into the cabin and embedded itself in the back of the pilot's seat. The engineers asked **NASA** about the disastrous results of the experiment, seeking advice on the design of the windshield and how the experiment could be improved next time. **NASA**'s response was just four words: 'Thaw the chicken first.'

Loopy limerick

An astronaut up on the Moon
Had a bright idea one afternoon
When he found a big switch
And so flicked it, which
Turned off the Sun – the buffoon!

Not so foul

Despite some of those fouler bits of space travel, astronauts are always in awe at what they see. The beauty of the Earth, the 'blue planet', can be stunning seen from space. Astronauts can also see human activity from space, like the lights from cities, pollution or explosions from natural gas mining. Then there are the other planets, our Moon and the stars that can be seen so much clearer. Convinced? Maybe it's time to book your trip. Yes, space tourism is already with us.

Space holidays

Even though the Space Age of human flight above the Kármán line 100 kilometres (62 miles) above Earth that marks the beginning of space is well established, very few 'ordinary people' have been up there. But things are changing. You may still get your chance.

More private spaceflight companies are offering civilians the chance to become space tourists. Only the very wealthy will be able to afford such trips to begin with, but as more rockets go up, prices will come down. In the 2020s, the space tourism market is expected to reach many billions of dollars.

If you'd rather experience zero gravity and pretend to be a space traveller without all the hassle of sleeping/eating/toilets in space, you might be interested in companies offering flights aboard a modified Boeing 727 that dives steeply to give paying passengers brief bursts of weightlessness. Such flights aren't actually space trips, but with tickets costing around $5,000, it might be the cheapest way to get a sense of what it's like above the Kármán line. And just think how you could show off to all your friends that you've experienced life as an astronaut by showing a selfie of you being sick floating in mid-air to prove it.

World records
(or 'out of this world records')

1 Anousheh Ansari from Iran became the first female space tourist in 2006 when the Soyuz TMA-9 capsule blasted off for a 10-day visit to the International Space Station. Ansari always dreamed of space travel and it is thought she paid $20 million (£10.5 million) for the trip.

2 When the space shuttle Endeavour docked with the International Space Station in 2009 it brought the total number of people on the station to 13, more people than have ever been together in space before.

3 Astronaut Tim Peake achieved a brand-new Guinness World Records title for the fastest marathon in orbit, running on a machine in a time of 3 hours, 35 minutes and 21 seconds.

Talking of Tim Peake...

This spaceman was the sixth British astronaut to go up to the International Space Station. He finished his 186-day mission there in June 2016. During his stay on the ISS, he researched new medical cures. However, he also had to help with the chores, such as vacuuming the dust on board, like all that skin debris floating around. He also took part in a spacewalk with another astronaut. The pair spent four hours laying cables, installing a vent and changing light bulbs. How many astronauts does it take to change a light bulb? On that occasion, none – the spacewalk had to be cut short when water got into his partner's helmet. The liquid probably leaked from the suit's cooling system. Three years before, a similar problem almost killed another astronaut.

Did you know, when Tim phoned his family from the ISS he made a mistake and called the wrong number and got through to a total stranger. Oops.

Limerick time

The astronaut Timothy Peake
Developed a super physique
To run at great pace
While weightless in space,
In a marathon – clearly unique.
(Undoubtedly Tim's at his PEAK!)

An astronaut known as Felicity,
When spacewalking drew
much publicity:
Somersaults in Culottes,
Got her tied up in knots...
From weightlessness and
great elasticity.

Wacky things sent into space

You never know if you'll bump into aliens in space. Now and again we've sent greetings and other things from Earth – just to say 'hello' in case anybody out there is interested.

In 2011, when NASA launched its Juno spacecraft on a mission to learn about Jupiter, they put three Lego figures on board. By having toys on board, they hoped to inspire more children to be interested in science and technology. The Lego figures of Galileo and the Roman gods Jupiter and Juno weren't the only toys to head into space – a Buzz Lightyear figure from the film *Toy Story* once spent 450 days in space too!

A car in space

In 2018 the super-rich American inventor and engineer Elon Musk launched one of the most powerful rockets with one of his sports cars on the top. It was the first time this type of rocket went into space, so he didn't want to risk sending something too valuable – just in case. It was his 10-year-old red Tesla Roadster with a dummy dressed in a space-suit strapped in the driver's seat.

Experts say the outlook could be grim for both the Roadster and the dummy (called Starman). They'll meet tough conditions in outer space. For a start, there's all that space junk, thousands of mini-meteorites and cosmic radiation likely to burn them to a frazzle.

Unusual visitors to space

 Luke Skywalker's Lightsaber (a prop from *Star Wars*) went up in 2007 with Discovery shuttle-flight mission STS-120.

 The ashes of Gene Roddenberry, the man who created *Star Trek*, who had his remains shot into space in 1997.

 A greeting in Zulu, telling aliens: 'We greet you, great ones. We wish you longevity.'

Bird poo

In 2006 the Space Shuttle Discovery was spattered with bird poop just before take-off. That would be easy to get rid of, wouldn't it? Wrong. During launch, the shuttle was sprayed with water and the craft accelerated from zero to 28,164 kilometres per hour (17,500 miles per hour) in just under 9 minutes. Despite all that, the shuttle was still splodged with white bird droppings as it blasted through space. You can never find a carwash in space, either.

Satellites

The more usual objects sent up on rockets are satellites. Today our lifestyle depends on these pieces of equipment hurtling around in orbit many kilometres above our heads.

Satellites come in all different sizes. Some communication satellites can be as big as a minibus and weigh up to six tons. Others that are used for short periods are only about the size and weight of a bag of sugar. The International Space Station is the largest artificial satellite currently orbiting Earth (about the size of a football field).

There are well over **1,000** working satellites whizzing around space – and getting on for **3,000** that no longer work. The oldest one has been up there for **60** years, but is now just another lump of useless space junk.

You might be surprised about what some satellites actually do:

1 Provide technology that supports our everyday lives, from access to the internet to banking services such as card machines.

2 Provide communications, including broadcasting television programmes and relaying telephone calls.

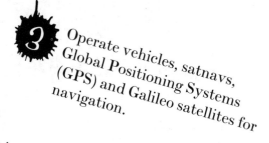 Operate vehicles, satnavs, Global Positioning Systems (GPS) and Galileo satellites for navigation.

 Collect information to help with weather forecasts.

 Carry out scientific surveys of the Earth's surface.

Make maps (and Google Earth).

 Spying.

Prepare to be amazed

If you put all the data that our satellites collect in a year on DVDs, they would form a stack nearly four times the height of the Empire State Building.

Did you know...

In 2012 satellite data showed that there were twice as many emperor penguins in Antarctica than was previously thought. Information from those 'spies in the skies' can help conservationists study many animal species and their habitats.

Satellites looking towards Earth provide information about clouds, oceans, land and ice. They also measure gases in the atmosphere, such as ozone and carbon dioxide, and the amount of energy that Earth absorbs and emits. Satellites monitor wildfires, volcanoes and their smoke, as well as other causes of climate change. Other important information can help emergency workers quickly respond to natural disasters.

Satellites that face out to space can do all sorts of jobs, too. Some watch for dangerous rays coming from the Sun. Others explore asteroids and comets, helping us understand the history of our universe. Satellites that fly near other planets can send back pictures and evidence of water, life and who knows what? The next great discovery could come any minute...

Did you know?

A satellite travels at over 28,164 kilometres an hour (17,500 miles an hour), depending on how high above the Earth its orbit is. It isn't powered with an engine but is, in fact, falling all the time by following the curve of the Earth yet never dropping to hit the ground.

Satellites very rarely crash into each other as each one is launched from a rocket into an orbit designed to avoid other satellites. However, as more satellites are launched into space, the higher the chance of one going off course. In 2009, two communications satellites (one American and one Russian) did crash and caused some red faces.

Rocket

science rhyme

Those satellites that whizz above,
We can't see where they are,
But all I know is my new satnav
Links up from in my car.
Where would we be if satnavs failed
Or satellites... what if?
We'd all get lost or steer off-road
Then hurtle off a cliff.

More Cheesy jokes

I've just had a new **TV** satellite dish fitted, but was shocked to receive a bill. I thought it would be free. After all, the installer told me that the satellite dish was on the house.

Did you hear about the astronaut who stayed up all night wondering where the Sun had gone? Suddenly it dawned on him.

I saw a strange pink campervan filling up at the petrol station and was sure it must be a spaceship as it had the letters UFO on the side. I asked the driver if she was some kind of weird alien, as everyone knows UFO stands for Unidentified Flying Object. She sneered, 'Don't be silly, it stands for Unleaded Fuel Only. Duh!'

A quick summary –

15 events in 50 years of space exploration

1969

The Apollo 11 spacecraft landed on the Moon and Neil Armstrong became the first man to walk on its surface.

1971

Russia launched the first space station called Salyut 1.

1971
Mariner 9 became the first
space craft to orbit Mars.

1973
Pioneer 10 became the first
space craft to fly past the planet
Jupiter.

1973
The United States launched
its first space station called
Skylab.

1976
Viking 1 successfully landed on
Mars. It sent back pictures and
scientific data for the next six years.

1981

The United States launched the first Space Shuttle, Columbia. The programme eventually launched 135 space missions over the next 30 years.

1986

Russia's Mir space station became the first consistently inhabited space station – remaining in orbit until 2001.

1990

The Hubble Space Telescope was carried into orbit by a space shuttle.

1998

The International Space Station (ISS) was launched into space.

2001

The **NEAR** Shoemaker (Near Earth Asteroid Rendezvous) made the first landing on an asteroid.

2004

The Messenger orbited Mercury.

2005

Venus Express (European Space Agency) studied the atmosphere of Venus from orbit.

2011

Mars Science Laboratory 'Rover' launched.

2019

Korea Pathfinder Lunar Orbiter (KPLO) is South Korea's first lunar mission – to orbit the Moon for one year.

Coming up — and going up

2020

A permanent Chinese space station is planned, and crewed expeditions to the Moon.

2021–2022

NASA will launch a spacecraft called Lucy to study Jupiter's Trojan asteroids. India plans to launch its first manned mission.

India plans to send a person into space on Gaganyaan by 2022.

110

2025

NASA to send back to Earth
material from the surface of Mars.

2026

Proposed launch of NASA's Asteroid
Redirect Mission (ARM), which will
see a crew in an Orion capsule visit a
captured asteroid in lunar orbit.

Early 2030s

NASA to launch humans into
orbit around Mars, possibly
landing on the Martian moon
Phobos and operating rovers
on the surface of Mars.

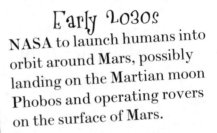

Manned missions to the
surface of Mars are aimed by
the end of the 2030s.

Proposed launch of Russia's
Mercury-P spacecraft, to
perform the first ever landing
on Mercury.

And finally...

3 cheesy rocket jokes

I got my friend a ridiculously huge rocket for bonfire night. He was so thrilled to light it and was over the Moon.

I bought some rocket salad the other day. It went off before I could eat it.

I launched my own clothing line this week. I knew I shouldn't have set up the rocket so near to the washing.

And a cheesy, cheesy joke

Astronauts mining the surface of the Moon discovered it really is made of cheese. They found a rich vein of the best brie, which they mined on two expeditions. NASA is about to send the astronauts back to dig out a third lot. However, astronauts have refused to go (and are really cheesed-off). One of them said another mineshaft would spoil the Moon, then burst into song with 'Did you ever see such a site in your life as brie mined thrice?' Groan!

Maybe Mars is made of cheese, too. As it's the Red Planet, it could be a giant Edam cheese! But this isn't a cheesy joke… Soon we'll find out because NASA's 2020 Rover mission will be equipped to investigate the rocks of Mars, as well as looking for past and present signs of life on the Red Planet. A core drill will allow the rover to dig deep into the surface to collect samples. Such research is planned for 2021, when it may also carry out an experiment to produce breathable oxygen from Mars' mainly carbon dioxide atmosphere. This could have major benefits for future manned missions.

Watch this SPACE!

The Foul and Cheesy Books Team expect Mars will actually be found to be made entirely of chocolate. After all, why is it that people look up at space and think of food – especially chocolate bars or sweets like Mars, Milky Way, Galaxy, Star Bars, Flying Saucers, Orbit, Magic Stars, Rocket Lollies, Space Dust… It's time for us to send an expedition into space to find if black holes are really made of dark chocolate. Anyone interested?

Final limerick

If you take the next
spaceship to Mars
For a holiday up in the stars,
Bring back souvenirs
In a couple of years...
Like genuine Galaxy Bars.

What happens
if you try to eat a Mars
Bar in space? You
choke-a-lot!

If you survived some of the truly foul facts and cheesy jokes in this book, take a look at the other wacky titles in this revolting series. They're all guaranteed to make you groan and squirm like never before. Share them with your friends AT YOUR OWN RISK!

If you ask me, this book is a waste of SPACE.

QUIZ

1. Which scientist developed important ideas about gravity?

a) Sir Newton Isaacs

b) Sir Isaac Newton

c) Sir Dmitri Dropalot

2. Who was the first person to travel in space?

a) Ivor Sputnik

b) Veterok Blastimov

c) Yuri Gagarin

3. What do the letters NASA stand for?

a) National Aeronautics and Space Administration

b) North American Space Agency

c) National Aeronautic Science Association

4. Which of these do you NOT need to become an astronaut with NASA?

a) To be able to speak Russian and have a scientific degree.

b) To be right-handed and weigh no more than 85 kilograms.

c) To be able to fly a jet, scuba dive and be super fit.

5. How do astronauts go to the toilet in space?

a) They don't

b) They pee through the window

c) They empty their bladders every two hours into bags for recycling

6. How do astronauts sneeze in space?

a) Very carefully

b) They don't – it's impossible to sneeze in space

c) They mustn't or they'll die

7. Who was the first person to step onto the Moon?

a) Buzz Aldrin

b) Pete Conrad

c) Neil Armstrong

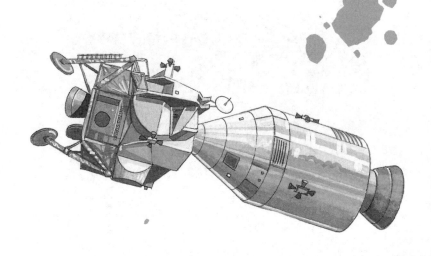

8. What has been used for growing plants in space?

a) Dirty pants and socks

b) Space dust

c) Lunar compost

9. What is 100 kilometres above Earth that marks the beginning of space?

a) The stratosphere

b) The Kármán line

c) The Cosmic line

10. Which of these has NOT gone into space (yet)?

a) A giant Dalek made of Lego

b) A sportscar

c) Buzz Lightyear

Answers:

1 = b
2 = c
3 = a
4 = b
5 = c
6 = b
7 = c
8 = a
9 = b
10 = a

GLOSSARY

Asteroid: one of the many large rocks/mini planets in space that orbit the Sun.

Catholic: a branch of the Christian church with the Pope as its head.

Comet: a bright object that moves around the Sun, which can sometimes be seen from the Earth as a bright line in the night sky.

Cosmic: relating to the whole universe (cosmos), as distinct from the Earth.

Meteor: material from outer space that enters the Earth's atmosphere and burns up in a streak of light.

Orbit: the path taken by one body circling around another such as the orbit of the Earth around the Sun, or a satellite orbiting the Earth.

Satellite: a machine sent up to travel through space to collect information and transmit signals.

Velcro: a fabric that can be fastened to itself.

INDEX

Look out for other wacky books in this series... if you dare!

I finished reading this Truly Foul & Cheesy book on:

........../........../..........